Mr. Crowford & I

A TRUE STORY BY GIRIJA NAVEEN
ILLUSTRATED BY ARJUN DEVADASON

Clever Fox® PUBLISHING
Chennai • Bangalore

CLEVER FOX PUBLISHING
Chennai, India

Published by CLEVER FOX PUBLISHING 2025

ISBN: 978-93-6707-174-8

ACKNOWLEDGEMENTS

This book is dedicated to my achan, A.P. Mitra Das -
You taught me to value the joy of simple moments.

A big thank you to
Arjun Devadason
The 10 year old "human energiser bunny",
who urged me to write this story and who did the beautiful illustrations

Naveen
'Idea - Generating, pixel perfect' pal and husband.

Sheila Appa
'Paragraph perfector' and a dear Friend

Nandini, Studio Arttitude (Chennai)
'Dream alchemist', who designed the original layout

Shrishti Selvam
For putting the book together

Don't know when and how Mr. Crowford and I came to be the best of buddies.
Oh, by the way, Mr. Crowford is a Crow – unafraid, extremely intelligent, considerate, generous, honest, mischievous and good-looking too.

Looking back, I think it all started when I used to watch him from my kitchen window, and noticed the way he would tilt his head to one side, stretch his wings, ruffle his feathers and deftly pick and eat the ripe neem fruit. I said to myself, that he really was a cute little guy, and wondered if I could strike up a friendship with this feathered person.

I placed a slice of apple on my balcony ledge and waited, without really expecting anything to happen. And sure enough, nothing did. I didn't give up though. I kept leaving a slice of apple in the same place every morning.

Then one day I noticed that the apple slice wasn't there! It happened again the next day and the days that followed. One day, I forgot to leave the apple for him, and my feathered friend perched himself on my balcony railing and refused to stop cawing until I brought him a piece of apple! And what surprised me even more was that he did not fly away. He seemed to know that there wasn't anything to be afraid of.

I was thrilled. I christened him Mr. Crowford.

Mr. Crowford loved his apple. However, one hot summer day in Chennai, I offered him a piece of cold watermelon, instead of the apple. From that day on, watermelon became his favourite. He had a specific place to eat his fruit. I would place the fruit on the right side of the balcony. He would pick it up, hop along the railing to the left side of the balcony and eat the fruit!

He was a very disciplined chap (birds of a feather flock together, I suppose). He would have 3 pieces of fruit every day. One in the morning, one in the afternoon and one around 5 in the evening, before he turned in for the night. Thus began, I truly believe, a unique friendship. We respected each other's space and never crossed the line.

Now, let me tell you about an incident that reflects Mr. Crowford's integrity and honesty – something that was beyond belief and so surreal. When the monsoon season began in Chennai, I placed little white pebbles, in my flower pots on the balcony, to prevent the soil from splattering all over the place.

A few days later, one very early morning, when I stood outside on my balcony, listening to the birds and soaking in nature, my eyes were drawn to the few empty spaces in the flower pots, where the pebbles had been placed. I didn't pay much heed at first. I couldn't think of anyone or anything, in their right mind, who would possibly be interested in a few pebbles, in a flower pot, on a second-floor balcony!

I just replaced them and went about my business. But lo and behold, the next day and the next, to my bewilderment, more pebbles went missing! Until one late afternoon, I heard the sound of stones clattering. When I went to investigate, it was none other than my feathered friend rummaging around in the flower pots, with a pebble in his beak!

I stood by the balcony door and told him that I was most displeased with his behaviour and that it was impolite to take someone else's things, without first asking. He looked at me with his head cocked to one side – it was as if he was trying to make sense of what I was saying. He did look so guilty and so adorable at the same time. I simply couldn't be annoyed with him. But I had to show him that I was displeased. So, I did not give him his treat.

I did so for 2 days, but then, I relented and restarted the fruit routine. At the end of that day, I noticed two pebbles placed in the very same spot where I keep the fruit for him. I thought it rather strange and asked my flabbergasted husband if he had left the pebbles there. His answer was an emphatic "NO". So, I just took them, washed them and put them away.

It happened again. But the next day there were 2 pebbles on either side of the balcony ledge! I picked them up, washed them and put them away. This routine of 2 pebbles on either side of the balcony ledge continued until a total of 16 white pebbles were returned to me!

Then it dawned on me that it was none other than my dear Mr. Crowford. All I know is that I did want to give him a tight hug. Mr. Crowford would have been terribly embarrassed for sure. But I just loved him more and gave him an extra piece of cold watermelon.

I think Mr.Crowford knew, how much we meant to each other. And he did something unbelievably special, to express his feelings.

One afternoon he was standing over one of the flower pots and cawing away loudly and rather impatiently, which was quite unlike him. So, I went over and stood by the balcony door. He kept cawing and looking into the flower pot as if to say "Take a look inside here". He then flew off and perched himself on a branch of the mango tree, just a few feet away from our balcony. He was watching me. I went over and took a peek. He had left me a chip of a beautiful ceramic tile! Gosh, I was speechless and so touched.

Our friendship continued for several months until one day something very tragic happened and Mr. Crowford never returned.

There isn't a day that I don't miss him. Each morning when I look up at the bright blue sky, I smile at Mr.Crowford, for in my mind's eye, I see him winging his way to lofty destinations – happy and buoyant.

I hope he knows that he will forever remain in my heart. His friendship has been the best gift I could ever have asked for.

Mr. Crowford's gift to me
- a beautiful piece of ceramic tile

I crocheted a border around it,
and made it into a pendant, to treasure forever

About the Author

The author is a retired travel consultant and a widely traveled individual. She enjoys meeting people, learning about different cultures, and has a passion for learning new languages.

In addition, she is deeply passionate about traditional crafts such as crocheting and knitting—skills she learned from her grandmother, who also instilled in her the guiding principle that "*A strong foundation is the basis*" and that "*Good enough*" *is not good enough.*

These values and the discipline they fostered continue to guide Girija in her work and in the many projects she has undertaken. With the same enthusiasm and passion, she is committed to passing these skills on to others, keeping the art alive for generations to come.

Her interactions with the younger generation are vibrant and engaging, and her storytelling ability is especially endearing—she paints vivid pictures with her words. One true-life episode, involving a chance encounter with a crow on her home balcony that blossomed into an unexpected friendship, inspired her to write this short and heartwarming true story: "*Mr. Crowford and I.*"